Your journey of reinvention and discovery...

... begins here.

This journal belongs to

Loosen your gaze

Full-Steam Imaginings

The ingenious beings of **Maxine Gadd's Zoologica** exist in a changed world that connects past and future, history and fantasy. Most are self-engineered, inspired by creatures who live in parallel zones or face comparable challenges. Others, like Koala and Meerkat, experienced powerful adaptations of consciousness whereby they now employ tools and mechanisms from the human world to navigate their altered reality. They are all resourceful, resilient and innovative.

This journal invites you to sit with these creatures and delve into their tales. Let them lead you into realms dark and bizarre, curious and playful. They may reveal treasure, alchemy and unusual truths. Underlying their tales is the triumphant fact they, like you, are intelligent and intentional adapters. Shifting sands, dissolving horizons and confounding discombobulation are met with graceful strategy, experimental tinkering and unflappable discipline. They look forward and become their future selves. Within the pages of this journal, you are invited to do the same.

Alongside the wisdom of this strange menagerie, you will find glimpses of other journals, real and imagined. Allow your journalling to intertwine with the ponderings of H.G. Wells, Mary Shelley, Jules Verne, Edgar Allan Poe and other esteemed character creators and world builders. Join them in exploring the stars, depths and insights of your imagination.

Be inspired to self-reflect or use the text bites included throughout this volume as story starters. Explore and add to the imagery to create your own realms and re-write their stories. All experiences are welcome here. You are safe* to express your crashes, your gateways, your monsters, your innovations and your bravest hopes. Whatever unfolds is part of a grand adventure. Creative self-expression can take you anyway and everywhere. Begin your marvellous journey today!

* You can write your secretest secrets in code!

Synchronise Your Watchfulness

Synchronicity unveils the intricate dance between our intentions and the universe's grander plans. Coincidences can be chance encounters or viewed as orchestrated events, akin to cogs aligning in a well-oiled machine designed to lead us toward our ultimate destinies. These synchronicities serve as guiding lights, illuminating the path to our desired realities. They also speak with immediacy to the opportunities within the present moment.

Picture this: you set forth an intention, a heartfelt desire, into the vast expanse of the cosmos. Like a beacon, it resonates with the universe, attracting relevant information, people, and opportunities into your life. Suddenly, you find yourself encountering references to your desires everywhere you turn— in conversations, in media, even in your dreams. This is the magic of synchronicity—a communication with destiny where you have a voice and a choice in the here and now.

The more attuned you become to these signs, the more they proliferate. Play with the magic of synchronicity and amplify your manifesting abilities through your journalling process.

SET YOUR INTENTIONS:

Begin by articulating your desires in a journal. Whether it's a dream job, a loving relationship or exotic travels, write them down with clarity and conviction.

ACKNOWLEDGE SYNCHRONICITIES:

Become mindful of synchronicities, from chance encounters to prophetic dreams. Record them in your journal to acknowledge the signs you are growing into, aligning with, and manifesting with authenticity.

HARNESS LUNAR ENERGY:

The New Moon is a potent time for manifestation. Invite this energy to charge your manifestation process by revisiting your journal and reflecting on the synchronicities you've experienced. Allow the New Moon energy to amplify your intentions and attract even more synchronicity into your life.

JOURNAL WITH JOY:

Have fun with your journalling practice, remembering that manifestation, expression and self-actualisation are creative endeavours. Add sparkles, cutouts, sketches, doodles, quotes and poetry to infuse the pages with vibrant energy. By weaving joy into your process, you amplify the magic within your intentions — whether inviting or releasing energies to your world.

By embracing synchronicity and cultivating awareness of its presence in our lives, we unlock the gateway to manifesting our deepest desires. In partnership with our higher selves and the unseen threads that connect us all, we can co-create a reality brimming with magic and possibility.

A Most Curious Treatise into Journalling and Pendulum Magic

A pendulum is a simple tool that can help unravel the energies that weave through every facet of existence. Even the ethereal spectres of hope, doubt, fear, knowing and desire cast subtle vibrations upon the tapestry of the universe. Within the enchanting dance of a pendulum, one can elicit a connection between conscious cognition, intuitive whispers and the loftiest reaches of one's higher self.

Through pendulum work, the delicate art of dowsing can be applied across myriad applications with an elegance both profound and mysterious. A pendulum is small enough to accompany you on any odyssey and can be improvised from the bounties of nature. A crystal pendant upon a gilded chain, a copper ring suspended on an unpretentious cord, or a needle threaded on a strand of cotton can metamorphose into effective pendulums as splendid or modest as one's fancy dictates.

There is no universal lexicon with which to interpret a pendulum's communication. Thus, our journey here begins with instructions on how to acquaint yourself with the language of your pendulum. Sitting with an elbow resting upon a table, suspend your pendulum five to ten centimetres above the surface. Around fifteen centimetres of chain grants your device the freedom to move autonomously. Any excess chain can be coiled around fingers or cradled in the palm. Aim for ease of posture to enhance energy flow and avoid having to adjust your position.

Relax into a light meditation by breathing slowly and deeply. It is then time to decipher the pendulum's choreography of affirmation and negation. Utter an unequivocal truth, such as, "grass is green." Observe the pendulum's movement as you maintain your contemplative state through relaxed breathing. Should the pendulum remain stationary, holding it over the palm of your other hand can give it more energy to work with.

Once you have noted the pendulum's response to a true statement, repeat this step with a falsehood. Proclaim an unassailable untruth, such as "kangaroos can fly", and note how your pendulum communicates a negative response.

Unwavering certainty in the veracity of your statements is paramount for the success of this exercise. Should you, for example, start to think about a certain airline and its flying kangaroo emblem, you may discover how your pendulum communicates confusion or a need for more precise wording. In this case, recalibrating your statement to "platypus can fly" will reveal the pendulum's negative response.

A pendulum might swing horizontally for 'yes', vertically for 'no' and in a circle where the answer is unclear. Other combinations might include clockwise, anti-clockwise and figure-eight swings. The more you work with and pay attention to your pendulum's movements, the more it will tell you.

Once you have identified your pendulum's affirmative and negative swings, the applications are endless. Before you ask for guidance, close your eyes and take three or more slow, deep breaths in and out. You may like to invite your truest self to receive guidance for your divine destiny. A blessing or affirmation can be a beautiful way to create a uniquely magical space for your session.

NAVIGATING THE QUAGMIRES OF DECISION-MAKING

When you are having difficulty knowing which way to turn, write your options in your journal. Rather than a list of options one under the other, write your options in circles or shapes across a two-page spread. If you like, you can brainstorm your list first so you know how many shapes you'll need on your page. Add an extra shape to represent an option you haven't yet considered or stumbled upon.

Move your pendulum slowly over the page, watching as it changes its swing in relation to each option. You may be given more than one correct answer. There is rarely one road to success! In this case, you can use your pendulum to investigate which path will be smoother, quicker, more enjoyable or the most likely to lead to meaningful friendships or other opportunities.

MAKING AN ORACLE OF YOUR JOURNAL

A completed journal can contain a burgeoning symphony of hope, disenchantment, contradiction, investigation, whimsy and meanderings. With a little pendulum magic, this sacred tome can become a vessel of divinatory guidance.

Suspend your pendulum over your journal and invoke its insight by uttering, "This journal contains wisdom that will help or heal my current situation." Gift the pendulum time to acquaint itself with the journal's energy and respond.

When the pendulum responds in the negative, respect its advice and try another volume. Should the pendulum bestow its assent, open the journal at the centre. Move the pendulum over both sides of the book to determine which half of the journal holds the insight that will help you today. Halve those pages and go back and forth until you identify the page or pages that hold your magical message.

A repeating pattern, a dormant dream, a past revelation or a poignant reminder of inner fortitude may come to light. Bathe in the luminescence of self-reflection. Conclude the divinatory process at your leisure with a moment of gratitude. Then, record your experience within the sacred confines of this journal as a testament to the mystical communion of pendulum and parchment to which you may return …

The remarkable creatures of the Zoologica have some strange tales to tell and quirky ways of expressing themselves. Some are complex and cryptic, others poetic and allusive. Welcome the unfamiliar and ambiguous as part of your journalling process.

Play around in other realms.
Try on different perspectives.
Discover new worlds of feeling.

Laying down the details and exactitudes may not be as
important as what you feel your story means to you at
any moment. Allow the message in your tale to change.
As the narrator, make it your job to champion the hero
in your story (the hero being you!).

Even broken in spirit as he is, no one can feel more deeply than he does the beauties of nature. The starry sky, the sea, and every sight afforded by these wonderful regions, seems still to have the power of elevating his soul from earth. Such a man has a double existence: he may suffer misery, and be overwhelmed by disappointments; yet, when he has retired into himself, he will be like a celestial spirit that has a halo around him, within whose circle no grief or folly ventures.

Mary Shelley, 'Frankenstein; or, The Modern Prometheus'

A fresh page holds the most possibilities, and an
approach free of judgement, preconceptions and
hypotheses will allow cogs to turn and sparks to
fly beyond your current awareness and consideration.

What seems realistic to you now is a false limit. Gaze beyond that boundary. The leap from comfortably attainable into daring possibility is much easier when you have a safe zone to return to. Anchor yourself to a quality or memory where you feel secure, then stretch into whimsy, fantasy and what actually could be if you made a tweak here or an adjustment there. The mechanics of change often involve adapting and fine-tuning existing designs. We rarely need to invent a whole new wheel – but when we do, it's always an interesting ride.

The inner workings of how and why we ascribe
meaning to something are mysterious, subjective and
deeply personal. A repeated image, a familiar phrase,
synchronicity or random memory can elevate the
mundane to significance.

Say farewell to two-dimensional progress, don your
night goggles, oil your joints, and bound upward.
The night forest is your playground. Your pinpointed
location may be unchanged, but your new height
transforms your world completely.

You carry more wisdom than it seems possible to have collected within the time you've had. This is the harvest of consistency. Every tiny lesson, revelation and gratitude compound to create a fuller sweetness that nurtures you and your endeavours in colder times. Ideas are pollinated, and connections and openings are made as you move from one golden source to another. Feel the warmth in your wings and buzz!

Leap with faith in yourself, knowing that on each
landing, you have the impetus to reach for the next
destination. And, when you fall, it is always forward.

Be confident in your ability to identify
the wonders in the weirdness of the world.

The plans you make are your own. Let them soar beyond what others deem you capable of. Your achievements may stun the hummingbird, but all the leaves of the grove will cheer, as they knew you as their own.

It is by luck and circumstance
that you know another way.

The year 1866 was marked by a bizarre development, an unexplained and downright inexplicable phenomenon that surely no one has forgotten. Without getting into those rumors that upset civilians in the seaports and deranged the public mind even far inland, it must be said that professional seamen were especially alarmed. Traders, shipowners, captains of vessels, skippers, and master mariners from Europe and America, naval officers from every country, and at their heels the various national governments on these two continents, were all extremely disturbed by the business.

In essence, over a period of time several ships had encountered "an enormous thing" at sea, a long spindle-shaped object, sometimes giving off a phosphorescent glow, infinitely bigger and faster than any whale.

The relevant data on this apparition, as recorded in various logbooks, agreed pretty closely as to the structure of the object or creature in question, its unprecedented speed of movement, its startling locomotive power, and the unique vitality with which it seemed to be gifted. If it was a cetacean, it exceeded in bulk any whale previously classified by science. No naturalist, neither Cuvier nor Lacépede, neither Professor Dumeril nor Professor de Quatrefages, would have accepted the existence of such a monster sight unseen—specifically, unseen by their own scientific eyes.

Striking an average of observations taken at different times—rejecting those timid estimates that gave the object a length of 200 feet, and ignoring those exaggerated views that saw it as a mile wide and three long—you could still assert that this phenomenal creature greatly exceeded the dimensions of anything then known to ichthyologists, if it existed at all.

Now then, it did exist, this was an undeniable fact; and since the human mind dotes on objects of wonder, you can understand the worldwide excitement caused by this unearthly apparition. As for relegating it to the realm of fiction, that charge had to be dropped.

JULES VERNE, 'TWENTY THOUSAND LEAGUES UNDER THE SEA'

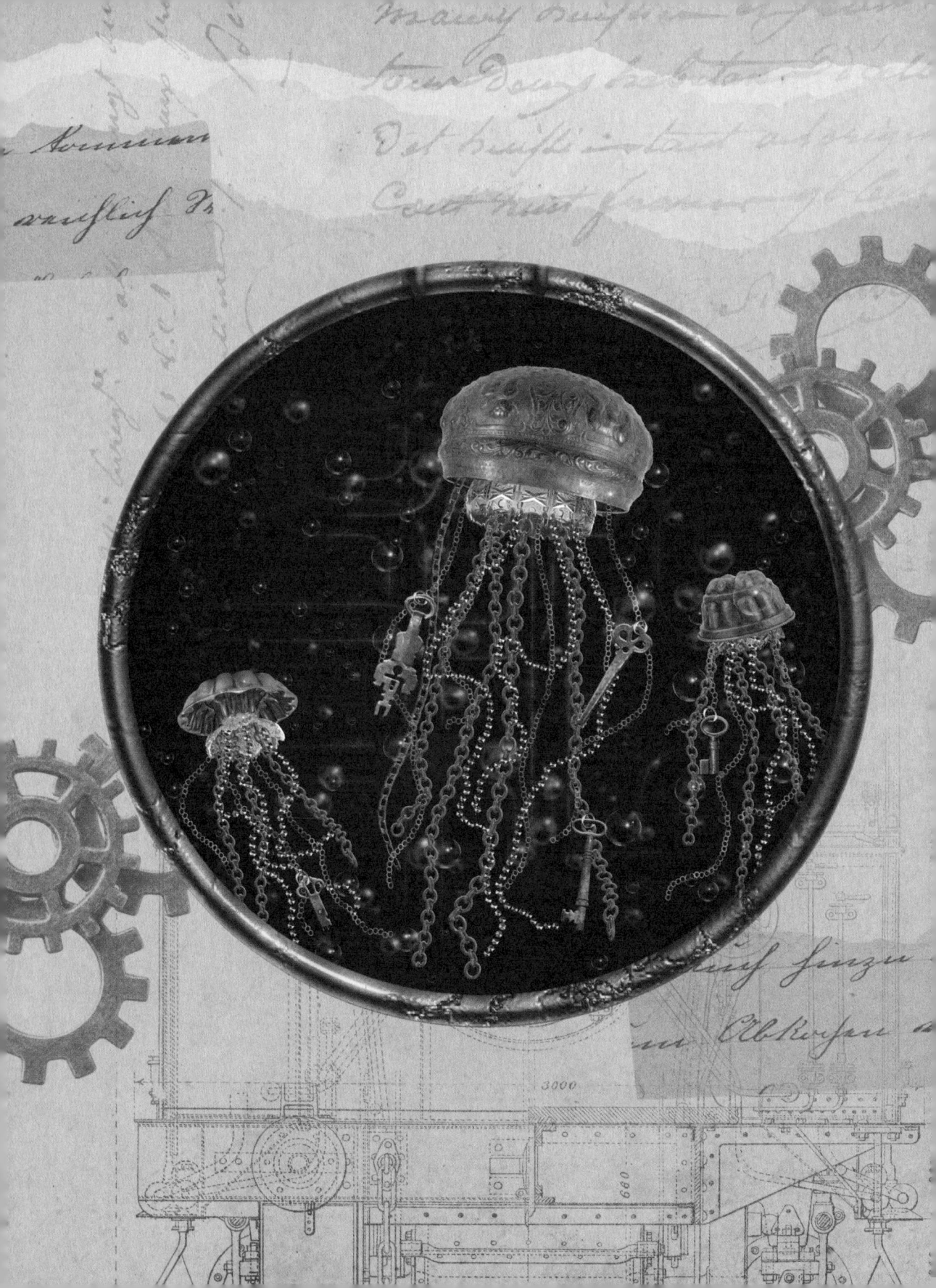

This is your world.

The tiniest errand is part of a grander plan, each delightful detail a mark of gratitude and every joyous 'just so' is a commitment to the moment and the momentous.

Your castles in the sand may be lost to time,
but their hope and reassurance endure.

This page is a pocket of safety for ideas and idealising, for secrets and doubts, for unburdening and reclaiming, and more.

Slowly, gently and surely,
together and alone, we are giants.

Genius takes time.

Bask in its leisurely unfoldment.

When you appear to be doing nothing at all,
the heaviest lifting goes on unseen in that
most marvellous machine - your mind.

The innovations, ideas and thoughts that spin
in one place cannot achieve lift-off. Move them out
of your head and onto the page where you can see and
feel them more objectively. Test drive them all!

March into the world alight
with purpose - emboldened by it!

At times, it may seem that you scarcely know yourself.
Everything is in flux, and so too, are you.

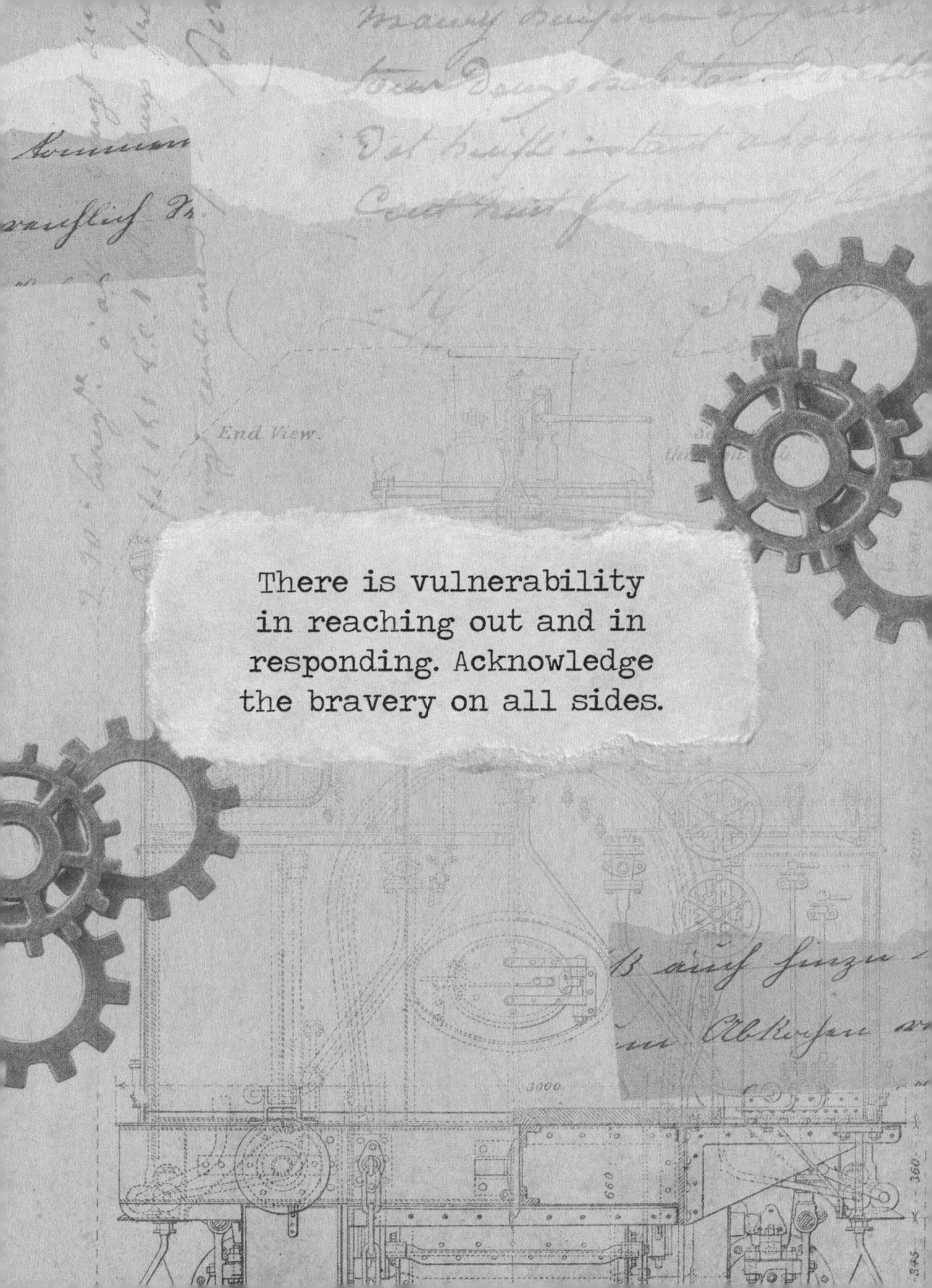

There is vulnerability in reaching out and in responding. Acknowledge the bravery on all sides.

Nothing is lost in your alchemy. There are times for lead and others for gold. The transformation from one to the other is neither false nor fixed. You can be either or both or something else entirely - depending on what a situation calls for. The real you is in control of that decision, and if the result is mythical, so be it.

Draw from the future to
propel you beyond the past.

All you need is a clue, one landmark
or constellation, and you'll know where
you are and where you are heading.

A fresh clue may hold the key to a cipher, so you revisit
past ground, discounting or bolstering theories or
opening startling lines of inquiry. While you can detach
from their influence, you know it is unwise to overlook
your emotions. They can hold the greatest clues of all.

I consider that a man's brain originally is like a little empty attic, and you have to stock it with such furniture as you choose. A fool takes in all the lumber of every sort that he comes across, so that the knowledge which might be useful to him gets crowded out, or at best is jumbled up with a lot of other things so that he has a difficulty in laying his hands upon it. Now the skilful workman is very careful indeed as to what he takes into his brain-attic. He will have nothing but the tools which may help him in doing his work, but of these he has a large assortment, and all in the most perfect order. It is a mistake to think that that little room has elastic walls and can distend to any extent. Depend upon it there comes a time when for every addition of knowledge you forget something that you knew before. It is of the highest importance, therefore, not to have useless facts elbowing out the useful ones.

ARTHUR CONAN DOYLE, 'A STUDY IN SCARLET'

BEING FROM A REPRINT FROM THE
REMINISCENCES OF JOHN H. WATSON, M.D.,
LATE OF THE ARMY MEDICAL DEPARTMENT

SHERLOCK HOLMES – HIS LIMITS.

Knowledge of Literature. – Nil.

Philosophy. – Nil.

Astronomy. – Nil.

Politics. – Feeble.

Botany. – Variable. Well up in belladonna, opium, and poisons generally. Knows nothing of practical gardening.

Geology. – Practical, but limited. Tells at a glance different soils from each other. After walks has shown me splashes upon his trousers, and told me by their colour and consistence in what part of London he had received them.

Chemistry. – Profound.

Anatomy. – Accurate, but unsystematic.

Sensational Literature. – Immense. He appears to know every detail of every horror perpetrated in the century.

Plays the violin well.

Is an expert singlestick player, boxer, and swordsman.

Has a good practical knowledge of British law.

When I had got so far in my list I threw it into the fire in despair. "If I can only find what the fellow is driving at by reconciling all these accomplishments, and discovering a calling which needs them all," I said to myself, "I may as well give up the attempt at once."

ARTHUR CONAN DOYLE, 'A STUDY IN SCARLET'

The alchemy is in your approach.

Plunging headlong into unknown and spiralling
burrows is all part of the treasure trade.
Should one wish to recoup lost, hidden or abandoned
jewels, one must go to them. It is not their business
to meet you halfway – not even part of the way.
It is by one's own efforts that treasures are found.

Do the stories in your midnight zone, the depths
of your consciousness, reflect your evolving insight
into the noble nature of reality? Challenge the
oceanscape of their intention, speech and action.
Hold them accountable to you. Crush the falsehoods
and cultivate nurturing beliefs so the ships that pass
are buoyed by tales of hope and illumination.

You would seek to change another being as much as
you would alter the colours in a rainbow. And you open
your senses to listen to the full spectrum of both.
The wallflower, the sea garden and the sunset are like
philosopher's wine. Savour them all, and feel the oceanic
connections of life in the quiet comfort of your soul.

The jewels you hide are keys to your hopes and talents.
Bring them to light one by one. Their many facets were
unremarkable in the darkness. In the sunshine, you will
see they are far greater prizes than you realised.

MAY 4, 1792.

The weather was delightful, and with a fair warm wind from the south, we made twenty-five miles before night. Today Thornton was sufficiently recovered to assist in the duties of the boat. In the afternoon he went out with me into the prairie on the west, where we saw a great number of early spring flowers of a kind never seen in the settlements. Many of them were of a rare beauty and delicious perfume.

EDGAR ALLAN POE,
'THE JOURNAL OF JULIUS RODMAN'

The absurd, the rational, and the fantastical are
co-existing companions, drifting and growing and
merging in and out of each other's tenuous outlines.

Go deeper.

In this vulnerable space, valuable lessons are grown. There is no scolding, "I told you so," only welcoming wings of, "I am here for you, I understand you, I love you."

There is an aspect of you that cannot be diminished.
It learns and expands and pushes against the
constraints of 'fine'. The ever-reaching you
strives for more – for something truer to you.

The chronicles that truly interest you are
not yet written. Be not defined but inspired.

"How would you like to live in Looking-glass House, Kitty? I wonder if they'd give you milk in there? Perhaps Looking-glass milk isn't good to drink—But oh, Kitty! now we come to the passage. You can just see a little peep of the passage in Looking-glass House, if you leave the door of our drawing-room wide open: and it's very like our passage as far as you can see, only you know it may be quite different on beyond. Oh, Kitty! how nice it would be if we could only get through into Looking-glass House! I'm sure it's got, oh! such beautiful things in it! Let's pretend there's a way of getting through into it, somehow, Kitty. Let's pretend the glass has got all soft like gauze, so that we can get through. Why, it's turning into a sort of mist now, I declare! It'll be easy enough to get through—" She was up on the chimney-piece while she said this, though she hardly knew how she had got there. And certainly the glass was beginning to melt away, just like a bright silvery mist.

In another moment Alice was through the glass, and had jumped lightly down into the Looking-glass room. The very first thing she did was to look whether there was a fire in the fireplace, and she was quite pleased to find that there was a real one, blazing away as brightly as the one she had left behind. "So I shall be as warm here as I was in the old room," thought Alice: "warmer, in fact, because there'll be no one here to scold me away from the fire. Oh, what fun it'll be, when they see me through the glass in here, and can't get at me!"

LEWIS CARROLL, 'THROUGH THE LOOKING-GLASS'

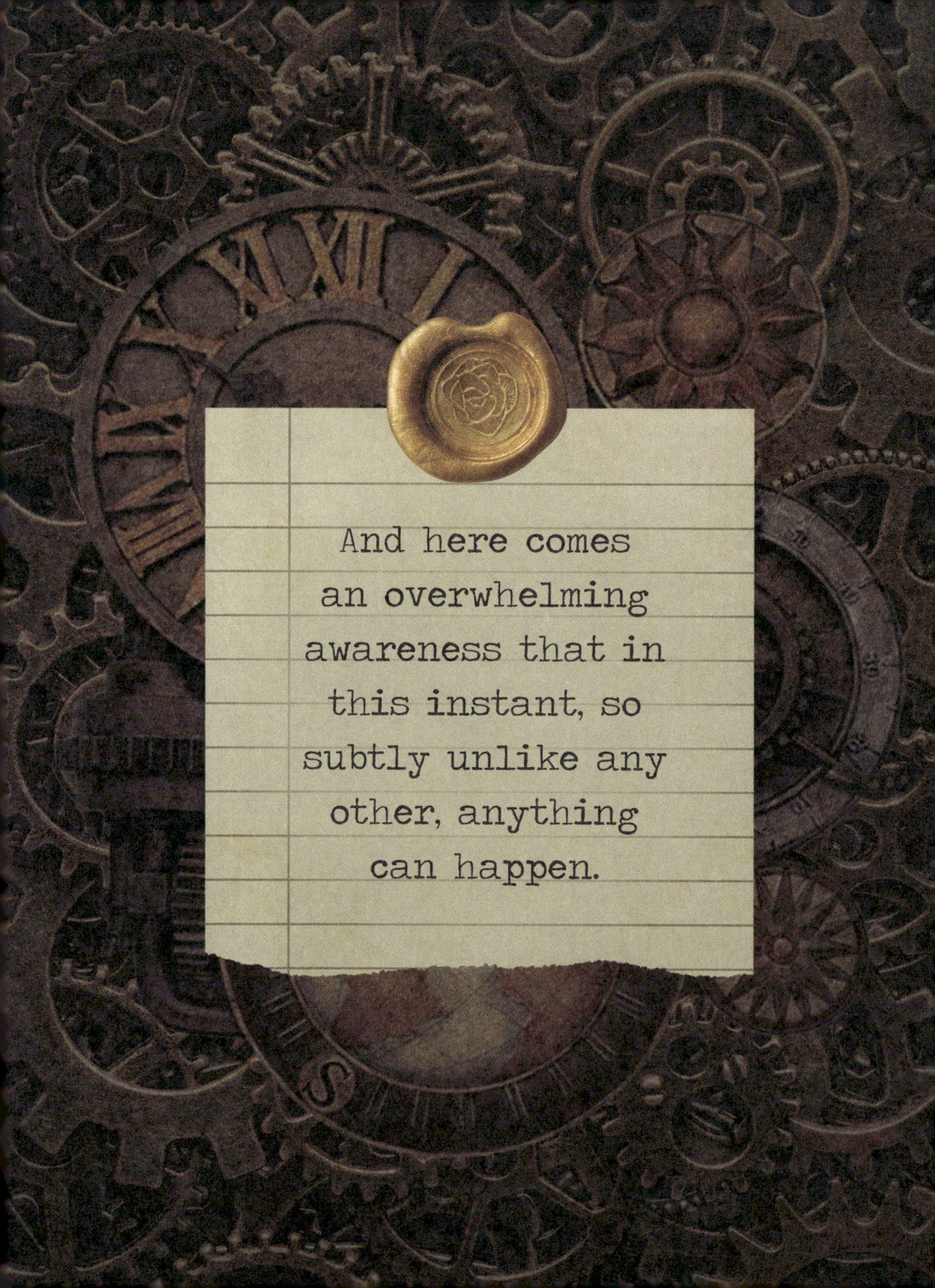

And here comes an overwhelming awareness that in this instant, so subtly unlike any other, anything can happen.

By taking in the true wonder of just
how far you have come, you can afford
yourself some rest. You are already whole.

Prying the truth from a situation
isn't always as important as recognising
its meaning. Myth, suggestion and feeling
can shape the future as much, or more,
than a sharply defined fact.

You can swim and leap and climb, and this brings you so much joy. It seems a strange suggestion that something is missing – something 'other' that would complete you and, at last, have you living happily ever after. And it is oddly fascinating that these suggestions are delivered with an air of benevolence as if the person most qualified to know what makes you happy is not yourself.

No one knows you as you do.

There's no need to feel brave, ashamed, guilty, defeated, bewildered, hopeless, sad, belligerent, alone, sorry or regretful. And there's no need not to. Whatever feelings come and go with the swirling tide are okay. Focus on the unchanging self and let them pass.

I told some of you last Thursday of the principles of the Time Machine, and showed you the actual thing itself, incomplete in the workshop. There it is now, a little travel-worn, truly; and one of the ivory bars is cracked, and a brass rail bent; but the rest of it's sound enough. I expected to finish it on Friday; but on Friday, when the putting together was nearly done, I found that one of the nickel bars was exactly one inch too short, and this I had to get remade; so that the thing was not complete until this morning. It was at ten o'clock today that the first of all Time Machines began its career. I gave it a last tap, tried all the screws again, put one more drop of oil on the quartz rod, and sat myself in the saddle. I suppose a suicide who holds a pistol to his skull feels much the same wonder at what will come next as I felt then. I took the starting lever in one hand and the stopping one in the other, pressed the first, and almost immediately the second. I seemed to reel; I felt a nightmare sensation of falling; and, looking round, I saw the laboratory exactly as before. Had anything happened? For a moment I suspected that my intellect had tricked me. Then I noted the clock. A moment before, as it seemed, it had stood at a minute or so past ten; now it was nearly half-past three!

H. G. WELLS, 'THE TIME MACHINE'

Thank the part of you that wants to keep you safe by trying to anticipate all eventualities. Thank it for its love and for striving to protect you. Thank it for alerting you to possible dangers and disappointments. Be grateful for its care and concern, and then acknowledge that trials will be ahead. Reassure yourself-all of yourself-that you are ready for them. You are an adventurer, and the truth is out there, waiting for you. Set forth and begin!

Life is precious, and hope is energised by laughter
and goodwill. People come in all shapes and kindness.
In a smile, some see a fool, others a sage.
And in both countenances, there is freedom.

Conversations and inspirations swim through
your mind in a mix of memory and things yet to be.
It's fun to play and replay scenes with different
characters and dialogues. They could all rhyme in verse
or move in reverse and have their fins painted yellow.
Oh, what an interesting time that would be. You might
paint it now or just look at some clouds …

It is not luck but trial and curiosity that unlocks
what you can do. (Yes, of course, a little luck too!)

'I wish they taught magic at school,' Jane sighed. 'I believe if we could do a little magic, it might make something happen.'

'I wonder how you begin?' Robert looked round the room, but he got no ideas from the faded green curtains, or the drab Venetian blinds, or the worn brown oil-cloth on the floor. Even the new carpet suggested nothing, though its pattern was a very wonderful one, and always seemed as though it were just going to make you think of something.

'I could begin right enough,' said Anthea; 'I've read lots about it. But I believe it's wrong in the Bible.'

'It's only wrong in the Bible because people wanted to hurt other people. I don't see how things can be wrong unless they hurt somebody, and we don't want to hurt anybody; and what's more, we jolly well couldn't if we tried. Let's get the Ingoldsby Legends. There's a thing about Abra-cadabra there,' said Cyril, yawning. 'We may as well play at magic. Let's be Knights Templars.

They were awfully gone on magic. They used to work spells or something with a goat and a goose. Father says so.'

'Well, that's all right,' said Robert, unkindly; 'you can play the goat right enough, and Jane knows how to be a goose.'

'I'll get Ingoldsby,' said Anthea, hastily. 'You turn up the hearthrug.'

So they traced strange figures on the linoleum, where the hearthrug had kept it clean. They traced them with chalk that Robert had nicked from the top of the mathematical master's desk at school. You know, of course, that it is stealing to take a new stick of chalk, but it is not wrong to take a broken piece, so long as you only take one. (I do not know the reason of this rule, nor who made it.) And they chanted all the gloomiest songs they could think of. And, of course, nothing happened. So then Anthea said, 'I'm sure a magic fire ought to be made of sweet-smelling wood, and have magic gums and essences and things in it.'

'I don't know any sweet-smelling wood, except cedar,' said Robert; 'but I've got some ends of cedar-wood lead pencil.'

So they burned the ends of lead pencil. And still nothing happened.

'Let's burn some of the eucalyptus oil we have for our colds,' said Anthea.

And they did. It certainly smelt very strong. And they burned lumps of camphor out of the big chest. It was very bright, and made a horrid black smoke, which looked very magical. But still nothing happened. Then they got some clean tea-cloths from the dresser drawer in the kitchen, and waved them over the magic chalk-tracings, and sang 'The Hymn of the Moravian Nuns at Bethlehem', which is very impressive. And still nothing happened. So they waved more and more wildly, and Robert's tea-cloth caught the golden egg and whisked it off the mantelpiece, and it fell into the fender and rolled under the grate.

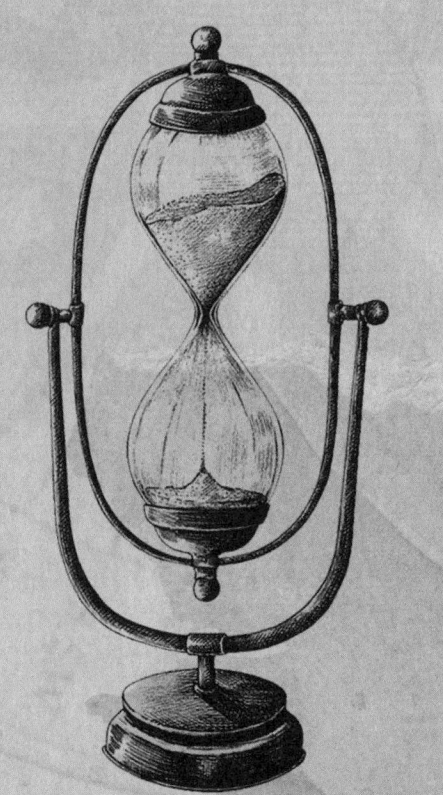

E. NESBIT,
'THE PHOENIX AND THE CARPET'

Wade into the world's awakening with
long, patient strides and the best of company
- your fresh, open, imaginative mind.

Flit and flourish in a space of your own
creation where fantasy rules.

In the soft glow of an open
page, action is ritual,
and words are incantation.

Your curious drive to understand, heal and be whole will triumph over caution and fear. Why wait?

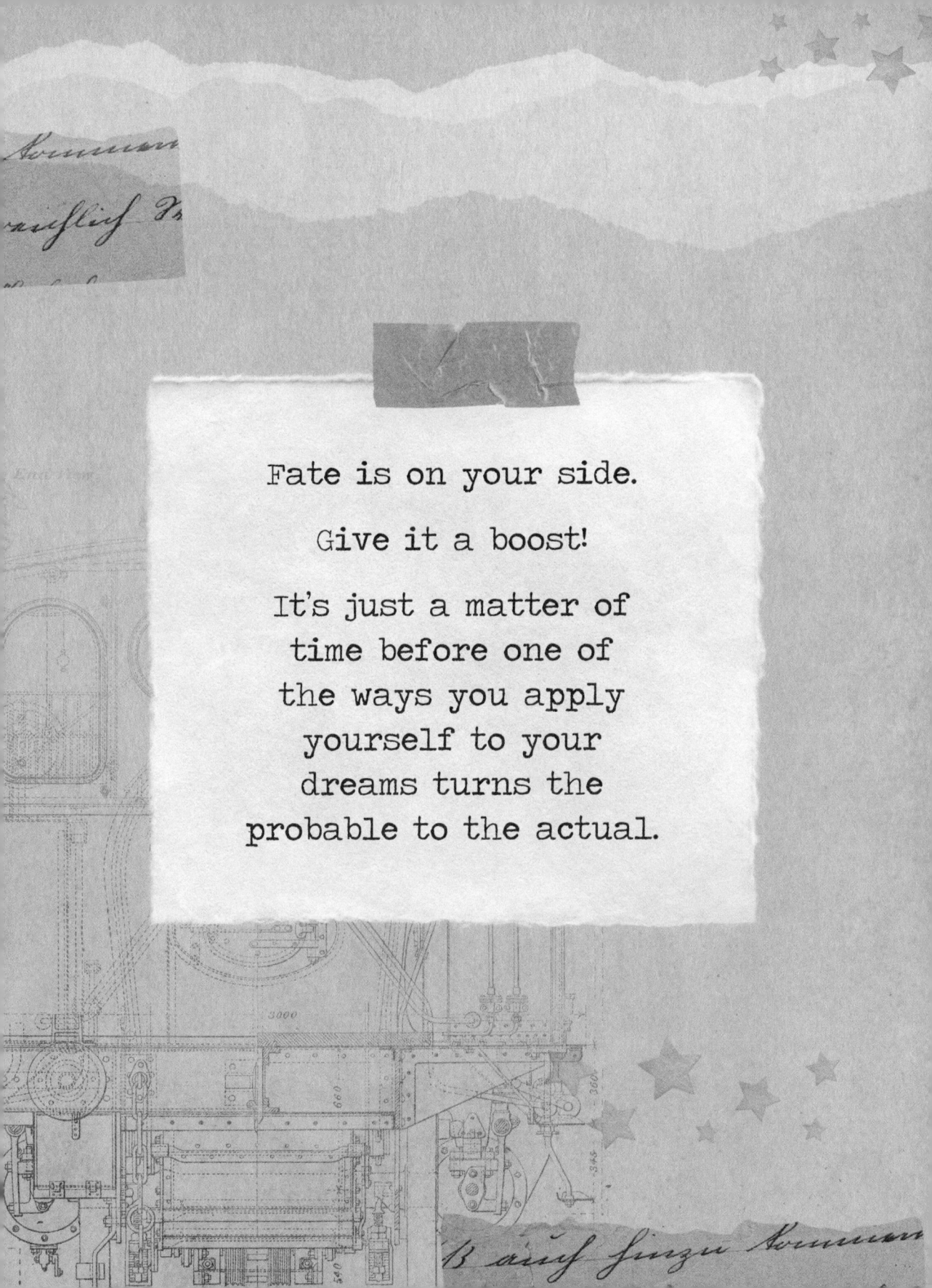

Fate is on your side.

Give it a boost!

It's just a matter of time before one of the ways you apply yourself to your dreams turns the probable to the actual.